Reconstruction

poems by

Walter Holland

Finishing Line Press
Georgetown, Kentucky

Reconstruction

ACKNOWLEDGMENTS

About Place Journal "Hermit Cake"

Special thanks to the following people who provided me with guidance
and encouragement and helped me in the preparation of this collection:
Jaime Manrique, Scott Hightower, Marvin Glasser, Deidre Johnson, Steven
Cordova, David Groff, Michael McKeown Bondhus, Kevin Hinkle, William
Johnson, my Copy Editor and Proofreader Brooks Becker, my Editor at
Finishing Line Press Christen Kincaid, and my dear husband, Howard Frey.

Publisher: Leah Huete de Maines
Editor: Christen Kincaid
Cover Art: Walter Holland. Monument Terrace, Lynchburg, Virginia,
Christmas 2016.
Author Photo: Howard Frey

Order online: www.finishinglinepress.com
              also available on amazon.com

Author inquiries and mail orders:
Finishing Line Press
P. O. Box 1626
Georgetown, Kentucky 40324
U. S. A.

Table of Contents

Introduction

THE LOST COLONY

RECONSTRUCTION

NATIVE SON

To Emma Smith and Billy Smith and the Smith family,
Barry Donald Jones and the Jones family,
Thurlow Evans Tibbs, Jr.,
my parents and sisters, Mary, Patt and Janice,
my friend Ann Riely Popper Jones,
and my loving husband, Howard Frey

And in memoriam of
Chuck Shull, Jere Real, Helen McGehee, Alfonso Umaña,
Kelly Hogan, Virginia Wiley, and Art Douglas

Reconstruction

"Some of the Negro servants left the plantations because they heard President Lincoln was going to set them free. But most of the Negroes stayed on the plantations and went on with their work. Some of them risked their lives to protect the white people they loved." And "General Lee was a handsome man with a kind, strong face. He sat straight and firm in his saddle. Traveller stepped proudly as if he knew that he carried a great general."

Excerpts from the official Virginia fourth grade edition public school textbook used in the fifties and sixties courtesy of Bennett Minton from his article "The lies our textbooks told my generation of Virginians about slavery,"
The Washington Post, July 31, 2020 at 9:35 a.m. EDT

Introduction

I was born in Queens, New York in 1953. When I was barely three months old, my father, who was a doctor, born in Manhattan, moved our family from our Hillside Avenue walk-up to Lynchburg, Virginia and a small rental cottage on Warwick Lane. My mother tried to acclimate herself to her southern neighborhood and make new friends. My three sisters were enrolled in a Catholic boarding school in town called Villa Maria and a short time later we all moved down the block to a large dark-shingled house at the corner of Norfolk Avenue. My father continued to prosper at the local city hospital, which had been built during the Civil War. My mother hired a maid as was the custom. We adopted a large sheep dog. Fresh milk in glass quart bottles were delivered every morning to our porch from the dairy just down the road and we lived next door to the Wiley sisters. Virginia Wiley was a high school English teacher and headed the drama department. Her sister Lib wrote for the society column of the local paper *The Daily Advance*.

As a boy, my life consisted of the small environs of Norfolk Avenue and the broad, elegant boulevard of Rivermont Avenue just up the way. As kids, we'd walk to an old bakery where ladies in white uniforms and netting in their hair served us southern sweets such as orange blossoms. A drug store next door, owned by a distinguished family in town, had a soda fountain. There we would order milkshakes or greasy hamburgers, our tiny shoed feet barely reaching the floor from the high leather stools. Down the way was Riverside Park, formerly the last stop on the street car line, though by our time replaced by city buses, buses to be avoided as these were mainly used by the help. A swimming pool in the park was for whites only and the hull of the packet boat that carried the body of the Confederate general Stonewall Jackson to Richmond was on display.

In the late fifties, my father had saved enough to build his own home in a new tract of suburban sprawl that had annexed a large plot of farmland. The street, Belfield Place, was a cooperative enterprise of a group of doctors. It reflected the burgeoning affluence of the New South, as more Northerners migrated to Virginia to enjoy "the good life." Next to our house was a barn with pastureland owned by Colonel Mosby. At the head of our street was an enormous preserve of land with a large brick colonial home, the property of Colonel Holt. The neighbors were all young white professionals and their young families were raised as part of the post-war "Boomer Generation."

As a boy I had an idyllic life with free rein of the wilderness behind our house, a beautiful pine forest that was interrupted only by the Norfolk & Western Railroad line, along which the passing trains provoked dreams of travel and adventure, as did the youthful promise of the 1960s.

My sisters and I were raised at a somewhat guarded distance from the local Virginia traditions. Northerners and Catholics, we were not of Old Dominion ancestry, but nonetheless my parents tried to accustom us to Virginian life. Lynchburg was the home of Jerry Falwell and many Baptist congregations and was rather insular and conservative, though some pockets of liberalism and progressiveness had begun to appear.

Little did I know that in *1954 Brown v. Board of Education* overturned *Plessy v. Ferguson*, the long-standing 1896 Supreme Court decision that upheld segregation and the doctrine of separate-but-equal. Nor was I aware that Virginia's Constitution of 1902 instituted poll taxes and literacy tests and mandated separate schools. But I could see that Jim Crow Laws persisted in Virginia until 1965. And I certainly was made aware of the long-resisted educational integration of Virginia schools in 1970, my first year of high school, when a race riot occurred after the all-Black high school named for Paul Lawrence Dunbar was abruptly shuttered and its students forced by busing to attend my predominantly white high school, E.C. Glass.

The poems in this book are memory poems. Many describe what I observed and felt as a young boy in the town. As my understanding and perspective continued to grow in recent years about my early life and the lives of my fellow Virginians, Black and white, I began to revise the poems, add to them, and expand them in preparation for this book.

THE LOST COLONY

Tobacco Shacks

(For William Johnson)

I used to count them on the side of the road, brown, abandoned walls, black tar roofing over wood, sometimes collapsing or leaning to one side, others already tumbled encumbered by weeds. Most of all the shacks seemed markers of history to me, and the mystery of Virginia's past: a life I never really saw, a century or more before. By my time the early encroachment of shopping malls, housing tracts, developments, had already begun. To me the shacks seemed bleak reminders of what I read as desertion and poverty, the crumbling of a dying way of life, not continued symbols of terror or misery or blood. Farm slaves cleared these fields way back, cut down the thick woods. Meadow flowers used to be everywhere; the land worked by a system of bondage. I used to visit a friend's farm out in Amherst County, tucked away at the foot of the Piedmont hills. He and I hiked to a slave cemetery with its old markers, limestone with dates barely visible, the rain having dissolved them, the run-off of winters, wearing away the carvings of birth years or death years. And just beyond about a half-a-mile or more, one solitary brick chimney showed where the main house had stood. And I remember another day long ago, venturing with my sister, stepping through the weeds to take a closer look and see what was inside those shacks, dotting the roadsides to our lake house. We stood on the dirt floor and took in its emptiness, no trace of life anywhere, just the heat of the air from the fields and the stray sunlight of afternoon. The buzz of flies darting in and out of the shadows. And I think now of atrocities and human tragedies that still must contend with uneasy silence and how nostalgia can act as camouflage, a sad, sweet and wistful sheen that covers a horrific truth beneath.

Main Street

1.

Here a statue,
a sentry to these empty streets, his fighting

battlements—New Market, Gettysburg—bronze.
All the way up the steep of the hill, the courthouse

sits in the summer heat. Jeb Stewart seized it after Richmond
was razed, the building's momentary glory, only days

till Lee surrendered. They set up a hospital on its steps—
blankets, plinths and bodies.

Once, in August, from the top of these stairs, I saw
a slow band of muddy water rise, the flood that struck

the stores downtown—the length of Main Street boarded up,
hardly a shop survived, the merchants have gone

and what once was—the spread of awnings shielding the glare,
the busy greetings, the trucks with guns—here men stood

with summer hats and maids at bus stops in oversized slacks
clutched at well-used grocery bags—their starched, pressed

uniforms—reeking of polish, Spic-and-Span—standing in the shade
of white magnolias, fumes from cars and buzzing bees.

Those lawns with boxwoods, spread, trimmed, and neat,
pineapple patterns that spoke of abundance, colonial insignias

of plantations and plenty, on screened porches the carol of voices—
old scratchy recordings, pedantic whispers, a chilly gentility

shaken in a glass, the warm amber of topped-off bourbon
a curious accent comes and goes in my voice.

2.

In the closed confines of a homeroom class, hearing the violent
chant over speakers—"death to Whitey"—public school—

loud confrontation, FBI men—overturned desks and scattered papers.
A lynching in the upstairs library—afternoon shots—sudden, fatal—

lawyers from the north—reports on the news—a quick settlement—
no one really knew who was innocent or who was guilty.

Yellow school busses moved up the hill, hauling Black students
from the "new" housing project, brick tracts in a hollow field

to books and boredom and "separate but equal,"—enlisted,
confined to Shop, Carpentry, Home Ed., Detention.

3.

My car would hurry past the downtown blocks of Fifth Street,
past the brick-red factory and the shooting hall, where men played

pool and fistfights flared and the smell of liquor hung in the air.
Late nights to late mornings, by the car dealership, the calypso

of bodies outside the bar—red-sequined pants and tight skirts hitched—
Wild Turkey, Ripple, or Southern Comfort, from the rear-view window

or the glare of the hood lone figures under the blinking lights
caught in the crossroads—confederates of night, slavery's wounded

bleary and battered, I'd gun my car and run the signal
past the slant-tin roofs with rainy run-offs, shrub trees over plain

metal chairs in grassless yards where ragweed thrived; there on Main Street
near a muddy river, barges to Richmond full of tobacco, riches

to produce the hillside mansions when the town could afford a theater for opera,
or moving pictures at the Warner Theater where I'd watch and hear from above

the laughter of "coloreds" at the matinees—who were they? Faces behind
beams of white—in the land of Dixie, that remarkable sight

of Pavlova performing "The Dying Swan" downtown—
white-feathered costume—plumes for her hat

a slender leg, pooled in the heat of one last spotlight—
culture for tobacco's kings—Caruso once sang at the opera house

for the town fathers exporters of clothing and makers of shoes,
stayed at the Virginian Hotel for a night where potted palms lined

the doorway and spittoons sat under ornate bars, Black porters
running back and forth.

4.

That tortuous road to Hollins Mill where men would buy
hooch in a jar and the jukebox played Black rock and roll,

the loud caterwauling of Chubby Checker and what came
later in "forty-fives," twisting music on a basement turntable,

buff of tires to a greaser's car, the gericurled hair of old Black men
who worked at Merriman's shop downtown.

In his barber's chair, you sat like a prince, doctor's son given a bench
as Merriman laughed and flapped his towel, buzz and hum

of the electric razors, smell of witch hazel or Barbasol, the greetings and grunts
of conversation—old Merriman dying of diabetes

or was it a stroke in the back of his car? Like Jackie Gleason,
brown and huffing struggling as he swept the hair from the floor

or stuck crisp bills in a pocket vest—a comb sunk deep in a sea of blue,
fished out by the pull of metal tongs, dripping of smells rank in impression

the cool feel of alcohol slicked on your hair, cut short in the military fashion.
Who knew where any of them went? The men who waited

by the porcelain chairs, staring in the mirrors near brushes for talc?
Like the shoe-shine men or the ones on the trucks

they left, gone home by end of day, beyond the suburbs
to the far away. The red-eyed man who stumbled toward our car

one sleepy midnight in the cross of a road
his look in the double white of our beam.

Ticket to Ride

(For James "Critter" Godsey and family)

A screened-in porch
where weeds of summer grow beneath TV towers
wild and uncontained. The red lights above, blinking,
carrying signals,
wealth and news for some.

In the single house with its four square rooms
where you'd sit in a chair strumming a tune
and your father snuck his beers
reading *The National Enquirer,*
the *Star*, singing the ballads
of Johnny Cash, Dylan, Seeger,
one dirt path to a bowling alley
down the hill.

What of that kitchen of simple things?
A jelly jar glass and some sandwich
spreads, your mother's laundry strung
to a line? He died in time of liver disease
and you, his boy, were never pleased
with small-town hopes and drunken fun—

you saved your pay from the movie theater—
projectionist in your high-up booth, made out
with the girls who stayed till the reel
finished—girls in the light
with silvery hair who wanted to go anywhere.
What did you see on the screen so bright?
Night after night,
the rolling attractions of a world beyond.

Your "show-biz" break was at the TV station
handling pets for a tired emcee; public service
for the city's pound. At the loading dock
with unfed dogs, you'd hang out smoking
joints and sing—

When the one broad field behind your house
announced the sudden change of spring
—you bought a ticket and disappeared.

Farmer's Market

The steel balances, tipping scales that hold
the spill of seeds, or soil-brown potatoes

under wooden stalls; near pick-up trucks and
open crates, the farmers hover with their

wives. Always a "slow" son or daughter
sitting in a chair who rocks and watches

and grins. Within the armory, hot coffee
with funnel cakes and freshly pressed cider. By late

morning, they'd all gone, the cavalcade of rusted
cars and wads of dollars rolled in cups, coins in

boxes for cigars. In that world of green leaf and
beet red, misshapen gourds or bins of corn

caked with heat and rain or dust, the smells
of tar-pitched fires from hogging sheds,

the curing shacks that smoked throughout the day
as hickory spat its sap. Stacked on fold-out tables,

the jelly jars, their hurried labels: "Apple Plum,"
"Tomato Sweet," "Mountain Cherry,"

dark or clear or boiled down to a thick amber.
Where women stood with homely faces,

open bags and marking pens, silver
crowns and lost teeth, babies in their cribs;

all things packed by noon, the men running their trucks
down the hilly streets, the stalls swept clean.

The Sundial

Its bronze face always cast with shadows
half in light, half in dark
the divided sequence of days which
revealed their markings—ridges

and incremental notches. I'd touch its ruled bronze pointer
encompassing the division of seasons,
resplendent lines and each degree
showing hours in roman numerals

as the sun swung above me, in that ancient
science of axis and old apogee. The snip,
snip, snip of the gardener, clipping Mrs. E.'s
flowers—she died of cancer, you know.

And ten years later, her husband was gone,
dead in their home for days, house lights
still switched on, his body found
half-decomposed—a heart attack.

How the days spin away from us, the sun
great and ablaze—those short meridians
the light makes, variable, hard to see
like glowing house lights in the bright of day.

At Evening

That conformity of evening
when women walked and men stayed

comfortably in their cars, or played golf
and drove home, after drinks; under

the lemon-colored awnings sat
one frail chattering matron in her chair

unsparing, she was, a survivor
of mannered restraint and studied charm

under southern light. All the town
blinded in sleep, with sauntering

turns of meandering speech that slowed to a drawl.
Sometimes when the mountains' blue

bled into red, I'd walk the avenue alone
recalling the boy who drove his car toward a wall—

a lawyer's son, spurned for a kiss—obituaries,
social notes, weddings, nervous fingers and pieces

of cake fed to the groom's sweet mouth. Living within
the affront of rules—how lonely one could be,

fitted to a world so heavily defined,
behind the closing of blinds.

Hermit Cake

Wrapped in foil on the cold back porch, the porous nooks and crannies
with honey, soaked in rum, the cakes turned black with nuts and berries,
candied fruit, desiccated, glazed and scented by cardamom,
or whatever else was dug from the bottom of the pantry. Heavy
and indestructible, the gooey preserves of a holiday at approach, another

soaked refuge for a teetotaler's rum. And the women who compared
their artistry, or failing that, the mere obsession for adding more,
adding like bits of words, the choked, broken parses of speech, gossip's
gooey subterfuge, the bitter they took from the sweet, the awful
comparisons and jealous green of the chewy, glowing condiments, red sour

cherries, and all that seemed scraps from their day's journey through
carpools and bridge and bean snaps in chicken salad served at the club.
Why hermit? Though to live withdrawn in perfume and negligee
silence, inside boxwood hedges at the edge of noon, was to show
their sweet, weighted burden under honey-brown skins,
their bodies baked under rays of coastal light, where husbands

rented summer homes, played adultery after hours, bored themselves with golf.
This mix as discordant as the past, layered black and nut, blanched white
in spun confections, jeweled globes, antique and dark resins stained as
wood, an admiring "awe" from the women at the tables who cut
through the hard loaf with a certain greed, each close-packed slice come of
infinite doting, a wedding treat meant to survive, fermented, acrid, dry.

The Pine Tree

(For Emma and Billy Smith)

It had stood perhaps a century or more,
we knew it was old and had been there since the land was a farm

with a sloping meadow to the stream. During the Civil War, Confederates had built
battlements, mounds of dug-up dirt, just a mere fifty yards nearby.

The pine tree had a split trunk joined at the base. The tree became buried
in winter when snow covered its branches

and bent some limbs clear to the earth. The birds found shelter and built nests
in it. The pine cones became Thanksgiving's center piece.

It brought me a certain awe, thinking about its age, imagining
its history and the many sights it might have seen:

carriages, pitchforks and musket fire. Perhaps it was a spot where rebel soldiers
camped, part of the wilderness in long unspoiled time

when the town had not spread very far and the fields were furrowed
running freely to the horizon. It sat at the edge of our driveway, my father

spared it when we'd built our house, found it a lovely touch, a nod
to local history. It smelled of resin and dripping sap and shed a scent

from its needles. Out our kitchen window I would watch it at dawn against
the morning sky, rays of winter sunlight casting long shadows

dappled in jeweled sparkling light. It marked the seasons for me,
helped me judge how deep were the drifts and whether school would

be canceled—my fervent wish. My mother used to scatter seeds underneath
to lure the sparrows and cardinals, drawing blue jays down below.

*

Later Dad called the tree a menace. Pollen, sap,
and needles, a threat to fall on his car as over time it had started to lean.

He chose one day to have it chopped down, sentimental though
it had become. So Dad asked Billy Smith, Emma's husband, to bring his crew of men

and saw the tree, branch by branch, slicing it into logs. He could haul it off
to the town dump or sell the wood for a fee. Billy was strong,

a man with bulging veins, curly crew-cut black hair topped by a mesh
cap which he lifted frequently to wipe his brow. Dark brown eyes and skin,

he wore a worn blue uniform that bore an oval embroidered with his name. I think
he worked as a mechanic, on account of the oil stains. The other men

seemed younger, and followed his knowledgeable lead. They wore
street clothes, hand-me-down sneakers. Billy had a winning

smile, and paced himself with steady determination, joked occasionally with the men;
but fell silent once Dad arrived. The second day they worked was Saturday.

It took all of the weekend. My father insisted I help out: use my muscles,
show some grit. But I could see the men were less than pleased, stopped from speaking

freely of girls or the lady they'd worked for on Ivy Hill. Billy worked hard,
lassoing ropes high in the tree, tugging its parts till they crashed to the ground.

His face perspiring and flushed in red, the heat affecting him more than the rest,
a handkerchief nestled under his cap. After an hour he'd call for

a break, lighting a cigarette while the other men crouched on the ground. I didn't know
quite what to do, felt I was little help, gathering branches with my dad's big gloves.

But Billy treated me kindly, like I was his young son, telling me how to pull
on the saw and swing the axe, though mostly he left me to the soft, easy stuff.

Little by little the men talked, relaxing in my presence;
teased the sullen man named Red, who drank too much, or so they all said, and Roy,

who had a girl up county. I felt slowly I'd earned their respect though they
kept their eyes looking down and steered clear of staring.

*

Emma came out with lemonade, my mother joined her, too. I saw our silver serving
tray and all the old glasses rather than the Dixie cups Mom had bought.

And Billy winked at his wife, her maid's outfit starched and pressed. By Sunday
there was only a stump and a little bit of sawdust left. The men were waiting

by the truck and Dad came out with Billy's pay. He handed over the bills.
One by one, Billy divvied them out and then walked over to me, dropped ten dollars

in my hands and gave me one of his grins. Then he climbed in the cab of the truck
and rode off up the street—dying of a stroke just a month or two later.

Mom drove me out to the Smiths' house. She'd wrapped some food in bright tin foil,
had me take it to the door. Emma was dressed in black and I saw a young boy

and girl tugging at her skirt and heard family voices coming from out back
as my mother waved apologetically from the car.

Jones Memorial Library

Corinthian white to tarnished yellow
the columns stood above the hill,

magnolias near a terraced vista, looking out
on Point of Honor, where John Lynch

made riches from his ferry, at the narrowest
section of river, tobacco, feed, housewares,

grain, the cargos hauled across or downriver.
Knowledge was a series of friezes, the carved

reliefs with serial names—Horace, Virgil,
Dante, Carlyle—to the town fathers, they

signified culture. Each terraced level
with their rising stairs, a spot for ivy

over broken glass, the globed lights shot out
by reckless kids—few went there—with its leather

volumes and odd assortment of antique prints,
down mildewed stairs to dusty stacks

the smell of molding maps and tomes, each folio split
a tea-stained color—in the reading room, hunched over,

alone, I'd read under the spinning fans, hearing the stamp,
stamp, stamp of the librarian's hand, arthritic, shaky

with her small, peevish eyes. Near the bust
of Cicero, the Confederate flag and one large case

filled with Indian heads, flinty artifacts with mineral
edges—I'd sit there for hours at my numbered seat

with my composition paper, my assorted pens
spread out and ready to write. What was the assignment?

An essay on the history of the Civil War?
The copied facts on Grant and Lee, the grim

statistics of the dead—Antietam, Bull Run,
Manassas, Shiloh—gray for the South and blue for the North,

the needless errata about muskets and swords, the sepia
photos and those men who bore the strange likeness to boys

at my school, their affable looks, thick locks of hair and faces
I'd dream about all through gym, jaws, and expressions—the defiant

gaze—almost amazed by the appearance of them,
as though they were living in the present day; parasol ladies

on carriage seats, picnic outings to survey the campaign,
driven from Washington just for the day.

Strange, if they only knew
how it would end, but then we never do.

In the sleepy hour of that musty
room, when all of summer hung close outside,

the slope of streets to lazy river, sunken flats near shallow islands,
weed-filled shores, as Black families sat on their corniced porches,

the Black men washing and polishing proudly their backlot used cars,
the good ole boys with Dixie flags raced their engines, swerved the curves.

Vestments

Father Finnegan has come to our class, is giving out
holy cards, smelling of liquor, the hard smell of
it up from his trousers to his ruddy nose—

on his breath, a whiff of bicarb. Say three Hail
Marys, he would whisper through the grate
and smile with his blue eyes, deep as marbles,

the tossed baubles of an Irish boy.
Though the nuns knew better, they held
his sleeves, or tugged at his cuff when he started to fall;

hurried him off, offering a prayer, holy cards
dropped as a parting gift, gold embossed from
edge to edge, uplifted faces and passionate eyes,

doves enshrined in glittering rays, from the bottom
of the chalice comes the glow of days, though
I try to imagine what giving can mean of the heart

to God, of the body and soul, the varied possessions
of life and breath. Father who blessed me at first communion,
then dropped the host on the carpeted floor, once in the homily

I heard him snore under the varied voices of the choir—
I thought of Joyce when I saw him kneel
on a winter night at the altar steps, something

of the exile and a poet's fear, the banished working-class
lad from Kilkenny, kissing the vestments of cold linen white.
The body chases the soul like a dog who chases its tail,

in that leaping moment before it's smacked—
no reason, altruistic or aimed, the smarting corporal
punishment, inflicted pain, the obdurate lesson of following

blindly, or at least obedience to a stern master—
lonely, idle, provoked and baited by the promised
call to reward. How docile he showed me faith could be,

but also hardened and real, like cold water splashed
to a face, the absolution by sweet cologne that covered
his body's acrid age; awakening to his flock again,

tending the small children who cried or bowed their heads,
all bleary-eyed he touched his finger to a forehead and blessed,
streaks of water in the sign of a cross, marks that confirmed sin and loss.

Oslo

A body white as the snows of Norway seen
in an eighth-grade film—

my love for the boy, born in Bergen,
just arrived.

Oslo's port, the ship and steamers hauling
their cast nets with fish—Industry, Commerce,

Products for Export—listening
to the old narrator on film—

as its thin strips tangled, moved apart, the looping
way of all desires continuously streaming

out of the mind, approximations in dark and light.
His towering chest and wan waist—

I knew him from the gym showers
after he'd return and stand by the tiles of wet white—

once stranded in a house in Richmond, a school trip,
 in my single bed I passed the night

not far from him, hearing his breath
and seeing the stone curve of his vaulter's arm.

What is the northernmost reach of memory?
Does it move with the weight of his form?

Year after year, in slow descent, the smooth
progression of desire's storm?

"Could have," "would have"—how the captains
guided their boats through the pale fiord

packets of letters to remotest towns—foghorn, sea—
then empty frame, sudden bleakness unreeling to the ground.

After Church

(For Anne Riely Popper Jones)

We counted cows and billboards
out where the mountains lay blue and long and lovely.
I never wanted more than that

for the rows of oaks and the waiting trucks
rings of holly hung on doors,
the white lines in the center of the road

dotting the gray for miles. To the West, Luray Caverns
and, worn of limestone, "Natural Bridge"—
"Natural Wonder of the World," where Indian flints

and moccasins were sold as souvenirs—
varsity pennants. Things seemed
uncluttered, barely a rest stop beside

just the tedium of farms and sheds
and the purple glow of clouds. Fireflies,
moved like sparks in woods and over creeks,

mountain laurel to pasture stones.
Gnats swarmed by my head. "Raise your hand,
Raise your hand," a gardener said, "flies rise to the top

and quit the face."
The diadems of milky weeds, Wild Carrot
among the burrs, the "purple heart," its tiny buds,

clustered there alone in white, cradled,
pulling away its filaments,
held like a bruise in my palm.

The rocky slope of a familiar hill, honeysuckle,
and cold air that clung near a stream. What of that underbrush
or the thorns, or even the pets I saw born, then later buried?

What is the message given? Stones of granite, slates
of gray and green limestone where I played and carved my initials—
those stalks I'd carried when it rained to keep me dry—

the green is gone,
the stems are broken. I've lived through much—how will I die?
Like a boy on a rainy path toward home?

The Lost Colony

Boys lined up to the right and girls to the left.
Separation

enforced until inside the classroom we'd puzzle over
our history project, a shadow box of the early

settlers, the lost colony of Roanoke Island,
colonists disappearing from sight—desertion, Indians—

Yellow Fever, the teacher told us no one survived
just sad markings on the side of a tree. Tame when

we consider Jim Jones in Guyana, his community
of followers drinking poisonous Kool-Aid, or the later

annihilation by AIDS, or ensuing terrorists
in a U.S. war. There in my box

with its pinhole opening, the cellophane end
and the makeshift stage

of cutout cardboard and construction paper,
trim shapes of English galleons, moving ships

on popsicle sticks near village huts cut out
and glowing. I held my box up toward

the sun, the silhouette opaque, glowing
behind—I have forgotten much

of this history. (I saved scraps of letters
from friends, postcards, stamps,

odd notes I'd hastily penned.) We move off
without address, in the box that someday becomes

our own—do all things show through as clear?
Do we find one world only to have another disappear?

The Crow

(For Marvin and Inge Glasser)

A sound of flapping wings, like stone to water
rippling, edge of morning's lapping—
this muddy red morning

wide
above the top of pines
lifting

springing back from the weight of talons.
Every morning awakened by the caw
in cold air or humid summer

motion and sight of spread wings
diving down to what? A shadow on a wall? The dead,
the living

flying with the call familiar?
Hovering years, black as silk,
spiraling down.

Once on a road ants crawled
through the remains of a black bird, looping their lines
on sinew and bone, open joints and white tendons, pointed beak

and bead of eye. With a stick,
I poked at a broken wing—
as it sails over air,

over roof, over house,
as it tumbles in the woods
it is sound

bound to stillness, sound gone
to black
and after.

Rays of Silver

(For Patt, Mary and Janice)

Close to the screen, outdoors, where moths
flew in the headlights, a cow pasture

hilly and covered in grass, the blaring speakers
over the noise of cicadas. Closer

near the playground under the frame of wood,
looking up at the moving beams from the projector,

waiting for the sun to fully fade so the feature
could begin. What figure?

San Francisco, Hitch's cinematic city
always in pristine white,

the Presidio with its sea-bright walls, the postcard colors of
Fisherman's Wharf, Americana of tinsel and red.

The schoolteacher and her repetitive lessons,
the sung carols by rote, then,

gathering, one by one, the black and shiny birds
appeared, each cut away and then return

revealing the flock, wire by wire, a growing invasion
underway. My sisters and I tried not to look

as the children hurried down the road, their getaway
a scant retreat, the pelting storm of angular

beaks. The paranoia of post-war conflict,
exposed by time. Seeing the birds now,

superimposed, their darting movements
carefully staged, the process

of combined effects—how fear could be made
by simple edits—sitting on the swings

while cars idled; the light of evening and the cool of air—
the birds so violent (like scenes I'd seen—

a room, my mother, mumbling, dazed,
scratch marks covering her arms—alone)—near Bodega Bay

and the gas station's flames, a careless match to set it
ablaze—how swinging below

the giant screen, our legs and arms pumped
toward the sky, caught

in the lighted beams
spilling through darkness.

Campbell County

Driving past familiar waysides,
no one about, but a sign

under the cool of a tree
advertising fruits and vegetables.

The car turns through the red bends
of fields and the small crisscross

of a town. Live bait and handy goods,
sale from a sagging porch. Delicate,

floating, thread-like Milkweed,
rushes through the open window

of the car. Bluebells and Elephant Ear,
wayside fields are covered in clover.

Going fast on the twisting road
past hundred-year oaks

and small plots of graves,
the sawmill shack
with its whine of blades.

Low mountains are circled
by clouds and hawks.

The final strange gesture of country
vernacular born of rugged pastures,
vestiges of wilderness,
collides into lakefront and lake.

Boats hum and there is the putter
of diesel where I stand, wet
and cold, elated to be twelve
and a fine swimmer.

White Collar

George at the bank
or Julian with the cars
in the showroom with shiny waxed sides and tags—
beside potted plants and lowered list prices—
Julian with his bid for city council, the home
in Boonsboro, the kids in school. Julian
with his milk at a quarter to five, three times a day
in a simple mug, no coffee or beer.
The car he sold all lemon yellow—
my first moment of independence
after the check
and the handed keys.

Julian behind the Fifth Street door
where Black men passed after buying liquor
where attendants labored in the oil-spotted lot—
Julian behind the cool of glass
entitlement given by the fact of color—a face,
a pedigree, a bloodline past.

With the power of destiny
I sat in the car,
showroom model—my father smiling—
my "bright future," as I turned the wheel—
unknowing the full terms of the deal.

Joe

Once the man who conjured
sex and women in a backseat, man with the broom
who swept and piled the trash of our clean thinking,
in a uniform,
he'd watch us in the parking lot, our sunlit cars
with roofs pulled down—

his talk of drugs
and nickel bags, as we'd giggle and take his hoarse advice,
"treat the women sweetly and you'll get a bigger piece
of the pie." Provider
of the make-out place, a pint of liquor, "cleaning supplies,"
whisperer of
bad thoughts.

With his influence of the "wrong kind,"
knowledgeable of our teenage fears
of the normalcy so much "expected." For what of school that kept
our heads spinning, and the trenchant talk of American might
and the Catholic catechisms and the short drives home
through affluent suburban neighborhoods.
Custodian of wiping away and making things look "nice,"
man of few prospects,
no real career or means, just purple shag on the seat of his car,
Marvin Gaye and six-track tapes—
Joe of the split lip and partly cleft chin,
whispering in the dark, half out of breath,
provocative, insinuating the devil's every whim—
"to get some you got to get in on the action."

Douthat State Park, 1960

The clear pool allows us to view rocks and all,
magnified under the currents of the stream.

Backdoor open to the car, wet swimsuits and ice chest,
the picnic in its foil. My sister, plastic thongs

on her feet, traipses about near the moving
stream, my mother at her side;

nearby, my father smoking his pipe;
this was their "good life": the station wagon, and chilled sodas,

West Virginia—mining country, still caught
in the vehemence of union strikes. Mildly

insolent, I wander, recite multiples, roots,
and sums; skim a dog-eared copy of *Life*,

dream in the forest of hills and creeks, the green waters
and needled pines, Christmas trees tapered and dark.

The radio plays all the way home, its talk
of the bomb. Floating on a raft in sparkling water

under the breaking sun, the forest succumbs to a fiery cloud—
lonely and uncertain, I drift—the sixties just begun.

At the Club

Waiting for the serve
listless to the slow dribble of a tennis ball
as it rolled from one end
to the other of the court—
indirection and strayed attentions toward
an instructor—boy of eighteen—
his brawny legs and sweaty brow—
counting off the minutes to finish the hour
when others like me—
his untalented charges—
were sent back to the tedium of the pool
our pent-up energies exhausted
by ducking his
volleys
brandishing our hard-strung wooden rackets
—plucking at the strings until he took
his break.

Talking over us and through us
as though our names were easy to forget,
loitering at the fence to watch the girls.

Hesitant to action
I lingered
more inclined to watch
the boys, who unflinchingly played at the game
hurtling about, aggressive, fast,
their moving waists
hard and swift—
the thud of balls,
their grunting labors—

this was the skill no one could teach me
the confidence of the attack, the swooping volley
with strong strokes and
pliant arms
these engines of unhesitant speed.
My clumsy motions
compared with their breakneck hurry.

What sweat revealed
through shirts of white, the spread contours of
panting chests—

chords of vein sprung from their necks,
the reddened flush of urgency.
My insecurity,
double-wrapped in a towel,
watching those courtly players
streak to the showers.

Cotillion

A scent of flowers—back to the fifties,
the last vestige of farmland before the suburban
sprawl—cold mornings of diesel and rail—
C&O flatbeds through mountain gaps—
some southern debutante who wants to get married

her gauzy dress crumples in my hands
and a mother's make-up runs from her eyes.
What is it? Sex—the smell of perfume,
a ballroom crowded with lanky teenagers,
white gloves and tight suspenders,

the boys who wear their hair long and favor
portraits of town fathers, white on black, silken
cummerbunds and sheen of tuxedo jackets. Flushed
faces touched by worry, hiding beers on the outside steps
or lighting cigarettes one flight up while mothers

spy from their chairs. Receiving line of preserved
smiles, that hopeful perplexity of women
who seem desirous of anything we could give,
like we were deer, leaping stags that stretched
and rutted in velvety coats, darting,

daring—her corsage presses to my cheek,
eye-shadow blue, hardly as alluring as the boys,
in shiny shoes, their slim trim bodies, drunken,
unruly, postures erect, zipping their half-closed flys.
Jostling, pinned with hothouse carnations,

their tallness and haughty stares. She touches my lips,
her store-bought smell, as the boys come and go before me,
bright, disheveled, tough. All of them restless in starched collars,
their broad necks, tugging to be free,
their shifting bodies hungry with need.

Forbidden

In my father's drawer
the folded shirts and cuff links
studded in brass,

the power of one day, buttoning and unbuttoning a collar,
tugging straight on a tie. This was how I imagined it.
In my father's drawer

the belts and socks and bottled colognes;
hidden at the back, a bottle of Bourbon,
deep underneath as though its contents

were obscenities spoken in a hush;
the things I was intended not to hear.
Daily on the trail—these little searches, the gathering of clues—

one magazine with half-nude figures,
a story of sex (Genet's fiction):
soldiers caught in World War II,

their secret homoerotic acts—
a French farmhouse, a fired gun,
the violent murder of the randy one—

I hurried off to read it alone.
In my father's study
rows of art books

prints of Goya's
rebels—one man's corpse stripped of clothes
the exquisite rendering of torso and line—

painting of Prometheus
chained and struggling,
what I wanted

to rend with my mouth,
vulturous as the bird, tearing
flesh from that smooth chest.

The Essay

Sometime around then you wrote your essay on the war
the draft board notice having come in the mail,
what did you say about pacifism and non-violent action?
Reading and writing what would be your defense, trying to build
conviction out of words on letter-paper stolen from your
mother's drawer. The war was just something short of high school

in your junior year, the call to enlist. What did your father think?
Having served in Korea, no advice for you, just left you alone
in your deep confusion (maybe he wanted you home),
those rumors rampant about conditions overseas, the escalation,
the deployment of troops at the D.M.Z.

Many defected and others
got high, that summer with their talk of the "freedom rides,"
war's confrontation merely spawning more—race riots, burnings
in Birmingham, the student protests against Vietnam,
still the town went conservatively on.

Relentlessly focused on the threat of the "bomb," the dangers
of Russia and a Cold War defense, while drunken debutantes
crashed through the fence that snaked the length of Langhorne Road.
Listening at the coffee shop to a few folk songs, sung by
locals who thought themselves "hip," loved Johnny Cash,

Baez, Dylan. What saved you?
Suspension of the mandatory draft, as the war
slowed down in seventy-one, no more reserves just college
deferments. In a matter of a day, it came over the news, you
were relieved from defending your views—would you have convinced

the board in the end? Three years later, those
back from Saigon, still hooked on drugs, the brother
of a friend, his upstairs room, said to be getting a job—
nightly playing the soundtrack to Hair, the day-glow
cover with psychedelic reds, swirls of green, what you took for rebellion.

Your legs filled out
and mustached chin. What did you make
of being spared? By the wayside highway you'd stop, stare
at the Blue Ridge Mountains in evening light. You wanted education
to set you apart, the secrets of culture, not the carnage of war. Gentility,

the middle-class comforts of wealth, you hated all of it,
those things you felt as false and selfish, not the sacrifice of art;
driving around town
in your father's car, living as politely
as you thought you should.

Country Club Evening

The golf course
covered with the glow
of twilight like a TV news program,

the commentary, lonely as a few evening stars
and someone who stands there—

watching the military strikes each night,
casualty numbers on a screen, and those scarlet
flares of rockets—the map of targets
and insurgents. I could only imagine

a ground hidden with detonators—
coming back from the dance

the girls in their dresses floated across the lawn—
how the punch had a ruby color

and the loud sound of the music
pounded out rock and roll—

driving the long way home,
there was nothing but night and trees

that retreated in the headlights—once defeated,
that world was to end, on the porches, in the den

the rumors of atrocities, the shutting of doors.
A confidence majestically breached

with that final acceptance of defeat.

RECONSTRUCTION

Reconstruction

(In Memoriam, Barry Donald Jones, 1950 - 2017)

Perhaps by the blackness of night
or the Blackness of you, the small

glowing aura of the smoking pipe
was seen as the barrel of a firing gun

or the menace of a criminal in the area,
a Black man about to flee on foot, though

you most likely had stopped, late night,
just for a smoke; a simple act to provoke

a policeman to shoot. With no ID
in your pocket, you merely disappeared

for days, the way Black men do in this country,
one more body in a bed hooked up to tubes,

"life-support," though the irony's clear
when you stop to think, few Black boys ever find

support. Black man come from the country,
a short ways off from Appomattox,

where a war for emancipation came
to a questionable end. No one knew who

you were, just your sex and color of skin,
and all the easy assumptions we tend to make

about those traits. You knew as nameless and troubled
a status as I could ever conceive, still maybe we both were

deceived all those years ago—me quite possibly more than you.
Or had you seen it all along and merely pushed ahead

by virtue of faith and the loveliness of country twilight:
red soil, rustling leaves, a wood house with a smoking

chimney, a meadow and a well. Burned down in the sixties
by a strike of summer lightning, the old homestead was replaced

by a series of temporary trailers set on blocks, heated by kerosene.
You planned someday to rebuild it, erect a two-story with a porch

and maybe beds of garden flowers, the same your grandmother planted,
primrose, forget-me-nots, hydrangea. The Christmas you had me visit

your mother baked her cakes and pies, a feast drawn from a wood stove,
layer-cakes of every size, foil-wrapped, next to ham biscuits,

placed on a giant folding table. So much was needed to feed a giant family: breakfast
was done in shifts, 6am, 8am, then 10. Lively talk and recited prayers.

*

So little prepared you for your future studies but your mother's
firm belief—you, a product of Head Start, a Great Society experiment,

how to instill success in those deemed disadvantaged—scholarship, hardship loan,
all paid by your church—bake sales and revivals, loose change dumped in baskets,

dollar by dollar, it grew with time, coming from those with less to give.
Groton, Dartmouth, Oxford, how does a country child, smart, gifted and Black,

prepare? Studies in Donne, Hopkins, Byron and Keats—French elocution,
recitations of Mallarmé, Baudelaire, and Verlaine. I was just a doctor's son,

product of that Virginian town, sunning myself at the country club,
taking parts at the Children's Theater, living in the leisure

of suburban life, northerner, Catholic, in the minority of that town
filled with colonial houses, serpentine walls, gates and ivy.

I didn't know or need to know about so many lives ignored
on "the other side of town"—arrests, bookings, Jim Crowe Laws,

back of the bus. What did I bring to your mother's table that
Sunday holiday morning? Hermit cake? Orange blossoms?

Brought in a bright white bakery box? I deserted you in the end,
or was it you who was forced to desert me? I never knew what

you'd seen in me. Such a riddle you were, inscrutable, and so compromised,
an anomaly from the beginning; so much pressure to succeed, be an example

of racial progress, smart, respectable, brilliant, articulate in faultless French,
though revealing sometimes your rural upbringing—foods you favored, homecooked

ham, down-home fare, fried chicken, rolls smothered in butter, and for breakfast
sometimes French Fries. Standing in the living room of my parents' home, white carpet,

cream-colored duvet, winged-back chair and silver trays, porcelains bought in
Japan, the ones brought home by my dad from war,

we were nearly the same age, but you were always a step above
—smarter, friendlier, generous, a talker with endless opinions, ever curious,

good at debate, you seldom needed to sleep, reading until 5 in the morning, staying up
most nights—Alice Walker, Toni Morrison, first one to speak their names.

*

The state trooper stopped you at the side of the road, locked-up until morning with just
a single phone call to your friend the judge,

who set you free of all the trumped-up charges. Had he not interceded, then what? One
more Black man harassed and doubted, profiled, "resisting arrest"? You thanked me for

inviting you to our place on Fire Island, paralyzed by depression, fired from your
teaching job—accused of sexual improprieties, though the details are still unclear—

some young man always answering the phone, telling me to hold, and then I'd hear
your cheerful voice—you knew that I was queer and I always knew that you were, too—

though having an "appreciation" for women, a "cocks-man," "having it both ways"
as your friend Garnell used to say—esteemed alum, Black man teacher, returning

to Groton as Professor of French—is there any other way but to live by division and
in division given you already stood accused of obtaining manhood by facetious means?

Sexual predator, Mandingo, dangerous miscegenation, playing the system before it
played you, smooth-talking liar, popinjay of Reconstruction, a conman risen from

a beaten South, charged with highfalutin self-aggrandizement—pretending you're
someone you're not—not white—not affluent—not sophisticated good company—

not a man of power or means. Barry, is this my confession? What could it matter now?
Dead as you are at an early age, sickened by years from that mistaken gunshot,

undeserved wound—over and over and over again—"excessive use of force,"
"under threat of harm," "I saw a gun." A split-second decision,

"the quick assessment of the situation," an act of self-defense. I cannot explain
any of it, though I was raised as you were in that pledge of allegiance,

that belief in equal opportunity under law, pursuit of happiness, rights of man,
civil liberty, separation of church and state, a whole decade of desegregation—

none of it ended in exorcizing the demon mindset, the racial division, the actions
of mean and hateful men. And so I mourn this bleak confusion, this paradox at play,

I miss your trenchant silences, the slow ritual of lighting your pipe, the rolled-down
window of "Nelly-Bell," that car, your sturdy pride-and-joy, taking the ribbon

of 29 South, rising hills and sloping hollows, speeding along while patting "her"
on the dashboard, talking of Aaron Davis, Jacob Lawrence, Beaufort Delaney,

Alma Thomas—Afro-American Art—and then the poetry of Wilfred Owen, Siegfried
Sassoon—your meetings with Anais Nin, your private open invite to read her papers,

visit her library. You knew your English Literature, could quote from writers
I vaguely read, had traveled the byroads of France in a small Peugeot

filled with native friends, then climbed on foot the streets of Mont Saint Michel.
So strange to me now, your secretive life on the "down-low," your prayer-filled

attendance at homecoming—revivals at the Rustburg church—gospel songs and "Praise
Jesus!" while also cruising the "Meat Rack" at dawn, that sandy forest on Fire Island,

saying you went to pick up trash, determined to "clean the woods," though we know
you went for sex.

*

You were always a body torn apart inside: riddled with scarring, ruptured spleen,
one-third of the intestines gone, shattered pancreas, lost kidney, diabetes,

chronic pain, damage akin to that in combat—years of rehab to walk, psych meds,
endless transfusions. They said it was "a miracle he survived." And what had been the clue

after the shooting to know it was you—a laundry ticket tucked in your pants
and a whispered name to a nurse, your sister's, over and over again,

in and out of delirium. Wed to a woman who took you for your settlement money,
dumped you when you started dying, come home to your family, a niece's empty

childhood bed, months in the care of church friends, family, seeing the young ones
grown up, till that Sunday morning—dead. Would you believe I'm wed now,

joined in marriage with Howard, still in pursuit of writing. Words, words, a chronicle
of what I heard, the long and short of my life observed, shut-down emotionally,

bouts of depression, though never deterred in a world that promised me safety
because of the color of my skin. Timid thoughts, doubts, regret,

a blind 50s and 60s nostalgia for a southern world, genteel and white.
Gone, though I remember our silent walk in the Blue Ridge, leaves sunlit and running

creek, stepping clear of the icy waters, mossy rocks and partial clearing—
you paused with tears in your eyes (nothing I'd ever seen before), filled with emptiness,

resignation, reporting your lost sense of self, your total loss of spiritual, moral,
emotional direction, what mattered, and what was to come, haunted

every day, every moment by that loud report
of one policeman's gun.

For Emma

Your hands pressed and folded our white lives
and tried to leave them perfectly uncreased

but so much was impossible to neatly separate.
I knew you knew the dirt that soiled

every facet of our intimate lives. Forgive me
for what seemed evident and known.

Aretha

One night returning on the Southern Crescent, to the old station
in Lynchburg, fielded by summer weeds and sumac trees,

to the cobblestone and brick rail yard where
solitary men and women went in and out of a neon-lit bar,

returning to the cool of clear evening, my father, merely a shadow
in his waiting car, I felt the migratory wielding of time,

my escape through the low hinterlands of night, farmhouses—
sleep—crossing bridges, trestles, and the miles traveled

from the grid-lit towers of the Northeast, returning over the humming
of wheels, smell of diesel, rain and stillness. Returning

alone, floodlit in the headlights of my father's car outside
the slow croon of its engine and the comfort of his organized

world. The town slept around me in wrought iron and ivy, its impoverished
streets oblivious to one more car that passed by off to the suburbs;

its spin of moths on the dark porches where late-night faces,
who'd known its legacy—yards near neatly trimmed paths—

way out or a way in to belonging, returning to what I knew of
urban blight, from boarded doors to Fifth Street windows

sailing past the ruins now of tobacco warehouses, the shoe-leather
factory, its thundering machines come to a stop in '63

the taped glass windows that once revealed faces, the workers
on their breaks, all vacant lots now and peach-red blossoms

still adorning the streets—her voice and only her voice on the radio
bringing the lonely claustrophobia and depth of those summer nights,

crepe myrtle moon and two drunk men before us in the headlights—
search beams supremely bright crisscrossing a divided world;

Aretha's soulful voice floating above the dark beauty of the fields. Her song,
a part of privileged green lawns and the rural fields and muddy roads

where roadside steeples hovered at sunset—churches with names like Bethany, Zion, New Canaan, Eden—her voice flares in the night.

Jefferson

(Poplar Forest)

Arriving to its brick and scaffolding
mid-morning's portico with bolstered beams—
what supports a roof? The edifice and
symmetry of democratic persuasions?—Jefferson—

a staff historian speaks of a statesman
returning on a ship, ambassador to the European
capitals, bringing to Virginia the agrarian message
antique desks and engineering, the synchronicity of writing pens—
inventions for a new pragmatic life—

am I part of this experiment?
Exile from British serfdom
foil for recalcitrant kings, homegrown variety
of Hobbes, Rousseau, or like that song of B. B. King
some coal-dark ballad sung in the holds
of subterranean dread.
There's a demon of Jim Crow that walks
with his pinch of snuff, struts the room of candles
while servants look away.

Who speaks to the man who loved Sally Hemings
and with her sired mulatto sons?
In the hall of peeling paint
the architects contemplate the beveled lines—
displaced foundations and bending floors
held up, warped by years.

A few spare tourists stand near fields
where corn grows in dispirited rows, more for show
to set the scene—what declaration is this?
In the cause of self-same liberties, pursuits
of pleasure
even now.

Man in a drawing room who would write
the blueprint for human rights—

framer of the Constitution, at what cost?
Caribbean financiers, captains of trade
bartering brutally for pickers, maids, imported fruit
from a Third World Eden. All eyes stare
at the White Father's hands,
his calmly rational study of books, his charted maps
and music stands, his pianoforte and gilded harp and the Chinese
vases enveloped by ferns.

Jefferson of the snow-white hair—
his colonial cunning—his association with
Dutch tradesmen beside their chairs
with brocades of velvet and vitreous things—doilies, cuffs,
embroidered lace,

architect of a faulty equation, inequality
for the few—
do I hold these truths?

Jefferson,
beyond you now,
from this porch, I survey the acreage, green with light, colonial
husbandry, yields of science—
the good of man—what
of your plans? Home of the brave.
Who serves the master? Who the slave?

Dead White Men …

Not the fortitude of founding fathers'
faces on a coin silvery smooth

collected and recollected, nickels tarnished,
the discolored back of Indian Heads.

Not the pale portrait of Washington's
head, Gilbert's painting in the National Gallery,

crossing the Delaware, his heroic stare
or Patrick Henry or Paul Revere, the speech

for liberty, the flight by night—
myths of freedom, stars and stripes while hordes of Coolies

laid down rail, the fated link of one golden
spike, men on horseback, sentries, trappers—

Remington's wilderness, roughriders, guns
and snowy wastelands, prairies of wind. Not

the likes of Dillinger or tough G-men, squinty
looks to smiles debonair, some cooing moll

who hangs on an arm, a half-clad Tarzan swinging
from trees through Hollywood jungles where natives

glare, their shoe blackened skin with curly hair.
What is the dour legacy of men? But the blank glare

of an untouched page, the spread of histories blotted
and doctored. Not "Birth of a Nation" as minstrels sang

or Vivian Leigh in a ballroom dress carried upstairs
by Gable's Rhett, who didn't "give a damn."

White

Not a soldier's monument
or its smooth base
columns of a portico with striped awnings
comings and goings and brief condolences—

Not the steps to a courthouse
and the rafters of noon
hot with summer
and stagnant air—

Not flowers of morning
and the beetle's rose, sweet and sickly as a sheet cake's
icing, printed cards with handwritten
names—

Not late snow
on a split-rail fence
where dead pastureland is rutted by a car
and wind gusts move through stunted pines—

Not a tee shirt blowing on a taut cord
vines of ivy steeped in the sun
some marble planters and a bright lawn
green to the corners of evenings—

Not the shade of an eye
around its pupil
blood-shot red to muddy-brown
one drunken look and a passive brow—

Not the color of suet slung from a tree
lard in its sack for marauding
beaks, or the hemp of a rope hung
and swinging—

Not the curl of smoke from a working hand
a Panama hat and burning cigar
the puff of cigarettes
from a truck with feed.

Not bowls of buttermilk
runny with flour, dusted countertops
and coated hands
rolling and mincing late in the day.

Not a chef in his hat with stacked plates
a rail car passing
with tables and flowers, a vase of crystal
and folds of linen.

Not powdered lime
on jades of grass
a bag of lye to kill off weeds
and bury the dead
under rings of stone.

Not the white of sugar
dissolved in a glass
dispersing in slow swirls of a spoon
the chatter of gossip from a back-porch step.

Not a laundry room with folded towels
a basement's sour smell of starch
stacks of shirts
and iron steam—

Not the sides of houses
in east D.C.,
postcards, tombs and honeycomb—
the capitol's dome on a still spring night—

Not the scratch of chalk
to a clean blackboard,
"The Pledge of Allegiance" written in class—
each ruled line with curls of script.

Not a father's shirts stacked in their drawer
Not the sheen of a car in a narrow drive,
the TV's screen as the picture fled,
a motorcade's honor guards, solemn, bowed.

Not the pale of my skin that burned each June
or the way I looked ivory and smooth
under covers of the bed
in the late of fall.

Not the downtown church with parishioners bored,
one solitary boy who believed in angels,
though he'd seen the photos of the burning cross,
the hooded figures fleeing
in the car.

The Balcony at the Theater

(Jim Crow, Virginia)

They were unseen, but their voices carried.
In the dark, they were the dark, not the screen's

images of innocence and experience, cartoons
of colorful imagination, the sweetly fabled, sparkling

scenes up there above us, but removed, retreating the narrow
steps that brought them to the furthest door, we rarely

saw them, just heard laughter. And in our world below,
its moral tales

so winningly simple and apparently my own. How did they
identify with that? Or was their kingdom less magic, their daily life

of feeling invisible, the transformations into comical
animals? The disparities so known

that while I waited for my ride, I saw the defiant way
they skipped up the street, making their way to that other

world, where authority was less clear and
never as contrite.

The Swimming Pool

Southern matrons holding toddlers by the hands,
leading them into the wading pool, as from the corner

of my eye, through the iron fence, the Black children
sat on a hill of grass, staring quietly, listening to our

laughter, the splashing and the clowning, the young
men on the high dive board, their bodies

the subject of my gaze. I was desirous
of their broad chests and their wet swagger

beside the sunlit pool, the focus of bored wives
who sipped their sodas with paperbacks

folded in their laps, lathered with protection to screen
them from the sun. That hour of noon, as maids

cleaned houses, waxed floors, took out
the trash. Gone now: desegregation's ruin,

hatred always winning in the South, whose legacy
of longing lies deep inside me, soil sinking in a buried

grave. The outdoor public pool bulldozed in,
a field of flowers with concrete at its rim.

We Shall Overcome

Born into that war, its melee on the screen, the choral whispers
of inquiring politicians. We shall . . . back to the integrated
high school where we walked past the barriers,

plain clothes officers cruising halls and the pins the Black girls stuck
into our unsuspecting backs. Gunshot murder of a student,
angry voices on a P.A. and the idea of Black boys playing in gym,

stuck in the back row of PE while we sang and cussed—
the special bleachers where they sat
like alien witnesses, strangers to our front row selves—

hormone-bound, restless, mad. We shall . . . recruitment in the cafeteria
ROTC, the draft board downtown and the bus loads of Freedom
Fighters in from the county, a Black preacher in his Coupe de Ville.

We shall . . . but we were overcome by fear and tear gas and the nightly
news, although I had hoped that college might spirit me
away; although I knew that those Black boys would all go to early graves.

For Anne Spencer

"Dunbar" was the Black school,
a "pile of bricks" on a hill.

Few drove there, most took
the bus, their flashy way of dress—

as she would make her way
past trellis vines of white roses, her writing

shed called "Edenkraal." This librarian
for the "Black cause," who'd scrawl her verse

on wallpaper patches preserved inside her
kitchen. In late of evening, taking to her garden

to read or pace or mostly write, the flowering
blooms in the half-light grew undiminished and dark.

The Birmingham Bombing

Photo of a mother arriving in court,
through her glasses, the face less willing—old—with an illness

that competes for her affection. Who triggered it, watching from afar?
Morning light in my room engulfs in yellow, like flame, and

the girls in white dresses who have become less and less, mere figments of shadows
sing in that wooden chapel, extolling, praising,

drenched in waters that affirmed salvation. Burning fire,
smoky leaves piled into mounds, cleared off in autumn,

less desired by my town's observant matrons, disordered migrations
of a lawn—unsightly scatterings brittle and brown—

what's burned out of me?
Was the killer the one who patted me on my head, said "son,"

and led me out into the world? Can I hear them, still praying for a second
life? The shouted gospels of each burning word. There is a way

I watch even now from an odd unease like the man who watched
it ablaze from his car—the way things were and still are.

NATIVE SON

North

There was something in that flight south, 1954 and a car,
the small motel on a highway of moths, the confines of 29

North of the city. What stars guided them, father
and mother, infant and girls? What riches? What safety?

A porched-in house and sleeping street, train cars
barreling night after night by the Westover Dairy

and the dingy creek. What of that quiet, steamy summer
with lonely strolls and hammock chairs, the southern town

with penned dirt yards? Did she dream of the Methodist Church,
the northern routes to Bear Mountain? How would she

raise her son? What beautiful vines would climb
the trellis? South was a meridian in the zone of slaughter,

the sloping gaze of sweetbriar fields, the gunning cars,
the bloodied heads. And this was the world I came to know.

Dutch Still Life

I used to favor the red of my mother's hair, Germanic,
Flemish, the fiery autumn along a Dutch canal, the far, dark north

where swallows dipped and flagons poured their moldy
summer wines. Her eyes were pearls of deft strokes,

my father's, more of the northern coast—blue of the sea
and miles of darting gulls over marshy flats.

Yes, this was the homeland, German fields near Hamburg,
I spoke the words, as trained in school, the odd vowels,

guttural, sharp but strangely easy, this native language
of philosophies, theorems, science, poetry.

A baker in Ohio, my grandfather, the humid ovens of dawn
or dusk, sugared icings poured over squares, the spiced drippings

with tiny beads like Christmas tinsel, sweetly spread; we were not
of the ruling class but tradesmen, merchants—tellers of tales—

in the end, I'm all that will finally be of that old medieval descent
seated alone under the darkness of an empty tree.

Purple Irises

(For Blanche Virginia Holland, 1923 – 2002)

Back when you were still alive, I joined you on one of your
strolls. Just home from college, I stayed at your house on Carriage

Way, where the townhouses had neatly trimmed yards, and the street had
lamplights fashioned to suggest the colonial past; white

clapboard siding and dark green shutters, each unit so like the other.
Not far off was the old highway, and beyond that the Blue Ridge mountains

silhouetted in pale blue. The highway plunged north, a corkscrew
route that twisted out of town until it dipped into a long valley

where the paper mill ran all day and night. As you were retired you
loved this walk toward evening up to the rise and along the white-picket

fence which bordered an open field, a field wild with weeds
and underbrush, wildflowers native to Virginia. Your arthritic knees

gave you pain as you walked and your once hardy body
had now dwindled to boniness, but nonetheless we made it

at sunset to the top of the entrance road. There a bed of purple iris
was growing in astonishing color, vivid and throated in yellow.

You said, they'd most likely bloomed overnight. They were so graceful
sitting there, graceful as you had once been, adorned in your jewelry,

your party finery, off to some lunch meeting with the women of the town.
Your hair was auburn red back then before it grayed. I remember your death

later, lying in an ICU bed, tubes disconnected, the room still, the orderly
waiting outside. But on that walk, you'd said to me how evening

was your favorite hour, the end of daylight, that golden transition
into night, when time you said seemed suspended and things glowed

in a lovelorn way— the irises brought you memories: sitting
on a porch in Suffern, New York, Adirondack chairs and thick fir trees,

the sturdy house made for snow with its stony thick foundations.
Your mother used to do her needlepoint waiting for your Dad to come home

from the foundry. Sitting there at the edge of autumn light, green shadows
and rugged trees, you'd watch the northern sky, its purple richness

edged in gold; sad you said was the twilight, the beauty of those last rays,
the way your father would trudge down the road,

his work clothes soiled, his face grimed, and how you'd
run to meet his arms, enfolded in happiness.

Afternoon, Lynchburg, Virginia

These roses flower
like the finery of women,
forties society women of drooping dress—
flowery brocades and frowsy hats,
stood over by the presence of men
their black ties and cummerbunds
squinty looks and squared jaws
an ungainly regiment—
defenders guarding themselves
from what?
Gone for more punch
or cigarettes, then off to the grave,
young escorts of Virginia's daughters,
with white gloves
looking upon me like a shiny spoon
silver-polished affluence
fit for a household drawer.

Now down these steps from a rose colonnade,
this terrace commemorates Virginia's brave—
Virginia, Korea, Vietnam—
southern sons in the course of duty
near small stone benches and summer's parched leaves,
the roses doomed to daylong heat,
a heavy scent, sweet and pervasive,
red, white, pink and dying—
like pillow embroidery
coverlets thrown over the arms of chairs, protective needlepoint
where the velvet wears—-
now, moved from town, after so many years,
that strange part of you, never expressed,
the odd sentiments, a world, which at best
struck a balance with pettiness.

Continental Divide

(For Bill S. McCraw and Seth E. Twery)

Light hit the van squarely in the center
on a sun-bright highway, snow at the glaciers,

white, quartz-like layers, shining downward to Denver—
earthen peaks reflected in the rear view mirror—

insects stuck to the sides of the van, legacy of miles
through Nebraska west, lost in a film of kicked-up dust,

receding plains. Here, arrived, crossing what to us was a teenager's
game, a puzzled map of the Great West,

a vast inland of stone and grass, the future, seemingly near.
On the seat a route we'd charted, loose-drawn pen-marks under magical names

wrinkled by the folds of last night's hurry. The three of us,
far from home. What your body offered, I could not have.

I wanted to cross the Great Divide—sixteen—sitting in the driver's
seat, all the way down to Taos in the heat, I watched the straight

and narrow of the road. Postcard of greeting—nineteen-seventy—three boys waving from a
slim wayside, the late canyons under tiny stars—though I'd rehearsed

what to say, I would never say it—at the brilliant ridge, where the peaks
shone strongest, we stood in our jeans by the snowfield's glare.

Winter Day

The snow would cover the bamboo and the porch
and fill the woods with drifts of white
The coldness in the oaks, a damp of air, glass
panes reflective, glazed in patterns of ice. The TV
glowed as the maid would stare, her working hands
upon the iron's grip and sounds of shovels moving on the road.

These were the days of winter still. The road
in heavy drifts that blocked the drive. The porch
screens whistling with the high winds. My hands
upon the window felt the cold and dreamed about the white
and sleeping woods as cartoon voices sang out on TV.
All of the forest behind that wall of glass

crystallized in patterns of cold glass—
watching from the window the fading white road
until the old movies began, flickers on a Zenith TV
or I was called to fetch the turkey, taken off the ice-cold porch,
pausing to blow my breaths of vapor, white
snow dusting from the screens as I'd pound with my hands—

frigid against wire mesh. Warming hands
inside the stove where bowls of glass
steamed and bubbled. The white
of light that filled the yard at night to the road—
the wind's howl across the porch
as I'd watch some science show on TV

the steady plumes of rockets to the moon, the TV's
talk of Russia and the Reds. Khrushchev's hands
pounding on a desk, cascading flakes across the porch
like fall-out drifting from the dreaded bomb—through the glass
and shavings of ice, beyond, a disappearing road,
our world so greatly constrained and white—

the talk of King, of "Blacks," "whites,"
wavering scenes of marches on TV
but no sign of my father returning down the road—
going to help Emma in her chores, her black hands
as she folded sheets, towels, blankets, filling her glass
with the water for the iron; the porch

so still, a porch layered in white
and my face pressed to the glass of the old TV—
its image of riots, fighting, upraised hands.

The Porch at Night

(For Janice)

Staring out the window, more adult these conversations,
hearing you in your thin blouse, pencil arms,
mascara, blackness pooling beneath your eyes.

Disheveled by indecision, sister standing at night
turned toward the fine mesh of the screens
where the thick sounds of the woods raged,

my mother—
what did she finally say? I only knew that you'd come back
from college, middle of the term.

This was the uncertain way things went in the world.
Bony wrists, spindly arms, loose clothing,
to prevent me from seeing

the truth, your late night visit,
a scant two hours,
next day gone to an unknown place. For days

you hung on an I.V. line, the snaking cord
in its steady flow, the only thing that
I was later told—"your sister refuses to eat"

All I wanted was to feel safe,
to finish my supper,
be smart.

Girls learn early to wait,
while boys hurry through their bodies
certain of growth, hardy to change.

Baltimore

(For Janice)

Seasons before—the blight of inner city
the winds of summer up Bolton Hill
and the marble stoops

where women gathered
before rain. Their tank tops
and bright white shorts, the rag-tag

colors of day. The North Market
with its stalls of dull gray oysters,
clamshells hurried into ice—

the fumes of factories low in the air
—at the hospital,
my sister in bed,

her car wrapped around a bridge,
her face sewn together, bone pierced by wire—
thin, gouged with tubes

she lay in that sack of spiral dressings,
a pale moth to her cocoon.
Her ruined eye condemning her as

seer, finally near her god
the dark avenging predator, depression.
Her pursuits temporarily suspended,

stopped by the necessity to survive.
A body, a canvas, piles of layered surface
that cracked in fractured patterns,

the scarring lines thrown to whitened arms.
A pulling back, torments, regrets—her husband
so devoted, but now old, his heart a borrowed thing

that ticks away, obedient to her.
Their cabin's interior, cast-off, a chaos without
care—the broken boiler bringing

only cold and through it all a desperate triumph,
an anger like poverty, a brilliance—
sworn to always serve, unsparing,

her obsessions (though where they lead her seem fruitless in the end)—
but so is art, and often, life.
Her house, a kind of disordered thinking,

a paranoia, which can scare—
a composition, dedicated, dark.
Damage seems evident in her work.

Art leaves her so discordant—each room
an accident—no recourse but to stand
—so little space to move

and every painting draped in cloth
like her body—hid
after treatment in the bed—

in pain—how she steps now to the edge
of purpose—of the brush
and all she nullifies.

Radio

Tuning in
to the static, a foreign voice
spoke through the glowing tubes;
turning the dial
in the dusty smell of the basement
a single bulb overhead
circling the desk in perfect light.
World War II, the Rosenbergs, Science
and the Bomb.
The lonely messages, voices in the night
traversing air
were fraught with implication—
clandestine maneuverings.

Power
was transformed
in circuits
like my heart
          in a burst of static interruption
     in amplification   distorted and young
  that odd interference   variant   bent   garbled receptions to a faint
noise, as my sister would paint
the vomitus of color over simple cloth
gessoed canvas to frames of wood,
the precision we built.

Flight

Duteous to his lessons of take-off
and landing, his excitement at leaving, lifted

high above the small green fields and farmhouses—
our house at the furthest remove, where she lay a figure

in isolation, those altitudes of sleep swimming white like her heavy
arms. In the locked ward she descended into worry, but that day so breezy with light

my father kept us level with the wind, the logic of instruments
and dials, the windows that promised the bend of mountains and rural earth.

Needles that spun, jagged as the ones that entered her vein and brought sedation—
he never explained, except once, the greater danger of liftoff and landing, how

floating above was the easy part, but bringing it down to the ground's long
narrow dark risked disaster. As propellers slowed, we felt the load

of our unsteady bodies and I saw how there was nothing
underneath to hold us up, but that stream, that rush

of force for ascension or fall, like the way she looked up
at me from the bed, as though I were not really there at all.

Nurture

In terrible whiteness
her body bloomed,
ruler of a dark kingdom
in obeisance to its charms
the spell that held us
trance-like—

Mother—you
kept me out,
my calls from the other side
seeking a way
into you,
forbidden and dismayed.

I fed upon your
nurture, darkness—
how luminous your voice retreats
in miles of shifting sleep,
emotion and its heavy milk—

as every piece of that despair
falls broken without form.
I was like a constellation
born by night and lost
at morning.

Appomattox

Going there with my sisters to stand
by the young man dressed in gray,
his uniform a rough imitation
and the milkmaid running from the rain—
did it rain all day? Or were we
in the house in sunshine, a parlor of surrender,

a careful arrangement of chairs and desk,
the ticking of a clock, McClellan's home,
set for the odd denouement?
Northerners come to live down south,
my scowling sisters, my downcast face
as the cheerful soldier continues to joke

and a woman describes the making of soap
and the blacksmith pounds his anvil.
On the ride home, my mother sits
sullenly tired, withdrawn, certain to take
to her bed, as I kick the back seat
and count cows—I want to hear the rumble

of guns in the fields and see the smoky
clouds from the fired flints,
hear why that house was chosen,
and wonder how two so divided
could have come together,
two so close be driven apart.

The Falls

(For My Father)

Toward spring we approach its base
by slate green waters and fronds of ferns.
The creek runs in a flat bed, wide and forested by rocks.
Above us,

the sky is blotted out by the fine
pale of leaves, whose shapes and variations, lined
and veined, create a canopy,
arching like the pillars

of some giant cathedral, high and vaulted,
quiet to its floor where in rounded mounds the moss
spreads in patches of quilted forms—
lichen straddling trees. Felled trunks

lay rotting in a heap.
Three decades back, you and I visited
this trail. Greens of one hue next to another,
vestiges of rotting bark and upturned layers.

Like loose tobacco in a store-bought tin,
the smell of wood and fermented things.
You carried me, toddler awaiting the sight of the water's
plumes, the crashing stream. Come to this very spot,

hand-in-hand, then bounding over a great
embankment, shelves of gray and white
barnacled rocks. Now at middle age
after many losses—you and I recollect

the way water fell furious down and the outcrops
stood polished in curves, hewn to the slippery spills
of cold. Both of us, near the rapids' current, cascading
jetties from cliff to cliff, pools trapped in

calm, the gentle tailspin—
descending in steady
deafening
sound.

The Luncheon at the Nursing Home

(For Virginia Wiley)

Annunciated in a voice of careful theatrical
projection, a rueful pause and then a quick aside,
Shakespearian, hyperbole and gossip, a maelstrom of
goings and comings, the great, late and classic, all
commanded from your seat where frailty is blotted from
your face, powdery with charm, the sugar-poured sweetness
of iced tea, a preservation like an open book's, that bears one mark,
only one, the dog-eared edges of age. You listen and greet
and musically misstep the answers too complicated to hear,
and fear, being old and removed, to soliloquize too much before
us, your last students—my tired, fully-grown presence
at your side. Though joined by an acquaintance—a Louisiana
matron, slipping toward the edge of ninety-three, her irrationality,
an aggravating guest—nonsensical and sweet, she ruminates
on travels long past, dates and details erased. Teacher,
always the teacher, you call this pupil back, with a gesture
as to say, we've had enough of tragedy and things past—
what about mirth, comedy and its brocade? Which worn well
"is always appealing" and points to things fortunate and future.
How the day brightens in this home where you stay, one of many
oddities and treasures—how the congregants with canes move
about the carpeted halls like extras on a busy stage awaiting exit.

At the Maid's House

(For Emma Smith)

Crossing your lawn, a drive and through a door
a Christmas tree, the white and gold theme, the embroidered
goodwill of some well-meaning matron,

for the black Santas and baby dolls,
the joy to show and display your family,
like gentry without a context, we arrive.

The room is filled with furniture and silver trays,
pans and photographs, frames which show your children,
smiling grown, your portrait as well with an Afro,

your only husband—gone—a stroke without warning.
He died, leaving you to your daily chores, the washing,
the kneading, the cooking—after lunch

you show us newer photos from a trip, a cruise
to the Islands, the wide assortment of relatives.
In a few photos you are resigned to smile.

Thoughtful woman you appeared looking through
a lens of meditative distance, not shyness quite,
but an old deference here, in your home, more

in focus, the clean, orderly atmosphere of mementos
and gifts. Thirty years to see this, to visit—
your house (once in a suburb built for whites),

the rolling lawns and ample garage, the grade school
just down the block. Now moved, you've arrived
and as always, fixed everything in its place.

Stacks

Putting away the books, my duty, through the aisles of shelves
past the smell of the homeless, past the radiator's warmth,

glossy books and the oversized, smudged and greasy, brittle spines
eyeing titles, reading some, rolling the cart across the floor

of sagging linoleum and wax, where idle women sat and cried
or pulled out letters from their purses, bundles of bills. And at the desk,

four laughing women, stamped each card, collected fines.
One with dyed red hair, another brown, the youngest one, who

always stayed, the head librarian who worked upstairs, constant
in gossip, her Tom Jones poster in the john. The one who never made

a fuss, died in her car, on Christmas Eve, a hasty turn, the other
felled by cigarettes and then spreading cancer. Always the rattle of my cart,

and how they'd taunt me with their jokes, so out of place, my college ways,
my New York life, day after day in their world of tragedy and knowledge

the flat, dull sound of the stamp, approving and disapproving, making old new.

The Pledge of Allegiance

My hand against my heart or so Mrs. Thomas
said, fingers spread apart, standing at attention

and gazing with my eyes upon the unfurled flag:
the bright colors of the town on a fall day: blue

skies high above the mountains, white clouds
gleaming in the sunlight, and red-brick porches,

sidewalks, walls, colonial and statuesque. Reciting
every syllable: ". . . one nation, indivisible, with liberty

and justice for all;" hearing that creed echo down the long
hall. Belief deemed necessary then, affirmation

of our civic call to duty and freedom in abundance; but not
apparent downtown or on the tiny lanes off Fifth Street,

with its sloping porches of rotted wood, plastic over windows,
tracts of dirt in barren yards. If you looked hard enough

as I did as a kid, it made you numb, quietly appalled
at all that neglect; a daily persecution, of those restrained

by the city's disgust; pristine environs, serviced by workers
at the back of the bus: the signs imploring one to hush

as they drove by the hospital (for white patients only).
In those recited words I praised the leaders

and the great gifts they endowed to our nation.
Unaware of what was still to come.

Then

Hearing of Stokely Carmichael and watching
the trooper's guns, hail fire over the heads of preachers,
the fat women with flowery hats, Mahalia's ladies—
cannonade of fire hoses
jetting streams into a crowd
and the foaming jaws of unleashed dogs—
half a city leveled flat
its brick lots in mounds of fire
with whispers of conspiracy—
who to believe?
Those impoverished avenues of downtown—
Victoriana stripped of paint
the warped wood and broken porches
how did a nation come to that?
Marauding sirens,
looters, guns—
from the shoeless children of Diamond Hill
as they batted sticks against a porch
to the concrete walls of Fishersville—
correction center for the errant poor—
spending their days without parole
while I stood before some smiling matron
took her candies into my palm, as antiques shone
from her airless den—
out of her mouth an acrid breathe
that spoke of death and godliness—
who was I, but
a Virginia son in a doorway
surrounded by cloying ivy—
now the looping calm of highways
and the democracy of malls.

The Appraisal

(In Memoriam, Thurlow Evans Tibbs, Jr., 1953 – 1997)

Your grandmother Lillian Evanti sang in Europe, her voice a veritable rarity,
a Black opera singer

who knew the classical repertoire. Culture was in your life blood. A rarity yourself,
a son with discerning artistic eyes.

With a mind for the arts, you were part of Washington's elite. The brownstone had
been in the family

since the early 1900s, brick façade and iron rails with stylized harps, the impeccable
downstairs parlor, and Lillian's

early collection of art. You made a living as an appraiser, combing the countryside for yard
sale treasures, people tossing

away old paintings, still lifes, portraits with broken frames, from the hand of little-known
Black artists, cheaply discarded,

and disregarded. And so your own collection grew: Henry O. Tanner, Aaron Douglas, Lois
Mailou Jones—all

hung on the stairway sidewall or spread upstairs in the house. To visit was to learn
of America's forgotten art, to see

without pretext of greed. So memorable your surprise, triumphant, exuberant
your green eyes

and beautifully handsome face—a Renaissance prince—the Harlem Renaissance—having
found by chance in cluttered garages

works so highly to be prized. You were wise enough to pay the two dollars—known
to museums and the refined circles of American art,

you willed your collection to the Corcoran. But love was difficult to find, and so you were
drawn to street boys, foster kids, drifters who stayed for a while,

then disappeared; offering them a glimpse at their true worth, buying them clothes, doing
them favors, teaching them that in art

there was no disparity, no limits of vision, no constraint on color. You were a sought-after
appraiser, a specialist where there were none before;

quick to fix a provenance, a name, a period, and to restore a lost authenticity. Stricken
in the end by HIV, you slowly wasted away, meeting

a suspicious demented end, drug vials emptied, music blasting, the bright lights turned on
everywhere; the culminating act of verismo, an aficionado of the aesthetic,

comes to his maniacal end, alone, collapsed, tragic;
still I recall scenes of a happier kind: standing at your sink in the kitchen,

wiping a cloth across a canvas, sweeping away its dark grime, to reveal its value,
redress the damage of harsh time.

Native Son

If there were claim enough
to deed the willful past

and let me go back,
would I take up that plow and dig?

Would the body appear again
unchanged? To swim the rivers of the boy

and languish on its banks. Would love
be anymore as tangible? Or hate?

These drum taps ensuing
along the faintest ridge—

no more, the valor of the living
only dying's cautionary song.

Walter Holland, Ph.D., is the author of three books of poetry: *Circuit* (Chelsea Station Editions, 2010), *A Journal of the Plague Years: Poems 1979-1992* (Magic City Press, 1992) and *Transatlantic* (Painted Leaf Press, 2001), as well as a novel, *The March* (Masquerade Books, 1996), which was reissued by Chelsea Station Editions in 2011. In February 1998 he received his PhD in English from The Graduate School and University Center of The City University of New York. His dissertation "The Calamus Root: American Gay Poetry Since World War II" received the 1998 Paul Monette Award . His article, The Calamus Root: American Gay Poetry 1945 to the Present, was featured in The Journal of Homosexuality. A subsequent article, In the Body's Ghetto, appears in A Sea of Stories: Gay and Lesbian Narratives in the Twentieth Century. He is a graduate of Bard College with a BA in Dance and Literature. At Bard he studied fiction writing with Mary Lee Settle and playwriting with Neil McKenzie. In addition, he holds an MA in Creative Writing from City College, where he studied under poets Ann Lauterbach and William Matthews. Poetry mentors have also included, Alfred Corn, Nancy Schoenberger, and Grace Schulman.

His short stories have been published in *Art and Understanding, Harrington Gay Men's Fiction Quarterly*, and the anthology *Rebel Yell*. A memoir piece appears in *Mama's Boy: Gay Men Writing About Their Mothers* (Painted Leaf Press, 2000). His poetry credits include *Antioch Review, Barrow Street, Bay Windows, Body Positive, Christopher Street, Chiron Review, Cimarron Review, The Cream City Review, Found Object, HazMat, Men's Style, Pegasus, Phoebe, Poets for Life: 76 Poets Respond to AIDS, Redivider, Rhino, The George Mason Review, The Harvard Gay & Lesbian Review, The James White Review, The Literary Review, The Piedmont Literary Review, Provincetown Magazine, William and Mary Review,* and many other fine journals and anthologies. His work has been featured on BBC Radio. Poems have also appeared in the British anthology of AIDS poetry, *Jugular Defenses: An AIDS Anthology* (The Oscars Press of London), and *The Columbia Anthology of Gay Literature* (Columbia University Press).

He was the keynote speaker at the First Annual Provincetown Poetry Festival in March 1999. In January 1996 he received honorable mention in poetry for the1995 David Lindahl Memorial Prize for Poetry, sponsored by *The James White Review*. He lives in New York City with his husband, Howard Frey, and writes book reviews for *Pleiades, Rain Taxi,* and *LambdaLiterary.org*. His papers have been archived at the LGBTQ National Archive in New York City. For more information visit: walterhollandwriter.com.

Also by Walter Holland

Poetry
A Journal of the Plague Years: Poems 1979–1992
Transatlantic
Circuit

Fiction
The March

www.ingramcontent.com/pod-product-compliance
Lightning Source LLC
Chambersburg PA
CBHW021152090426
42740CB00008B/1053